PRESCHOOL WORKBOOK ZONE

ALPHABET - SUDOKU - DOT TO DOT
AND MUCH MORE..

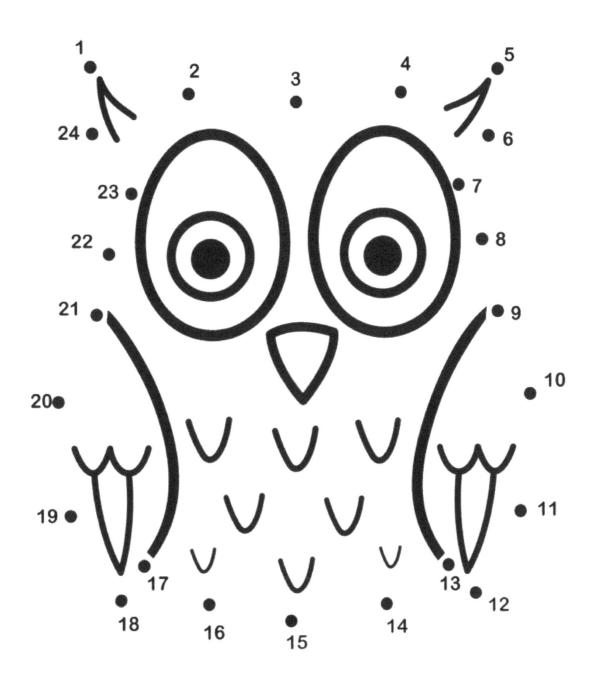

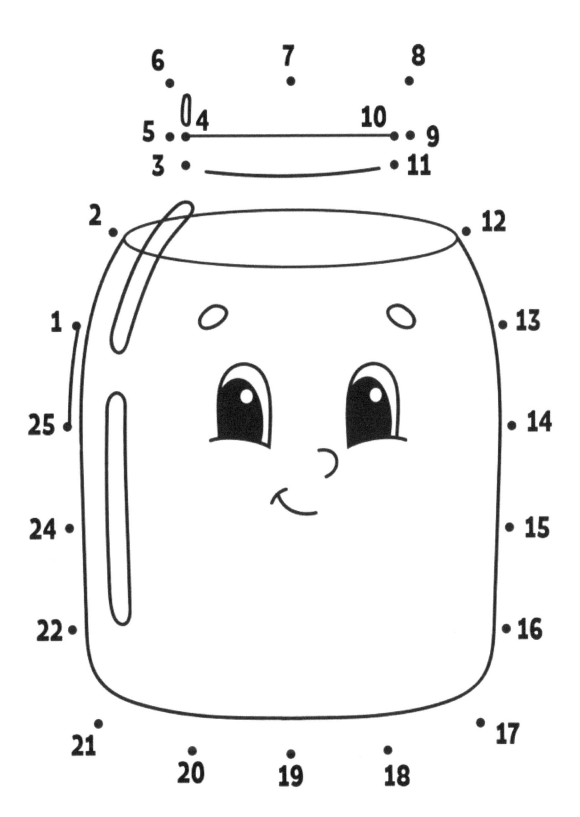

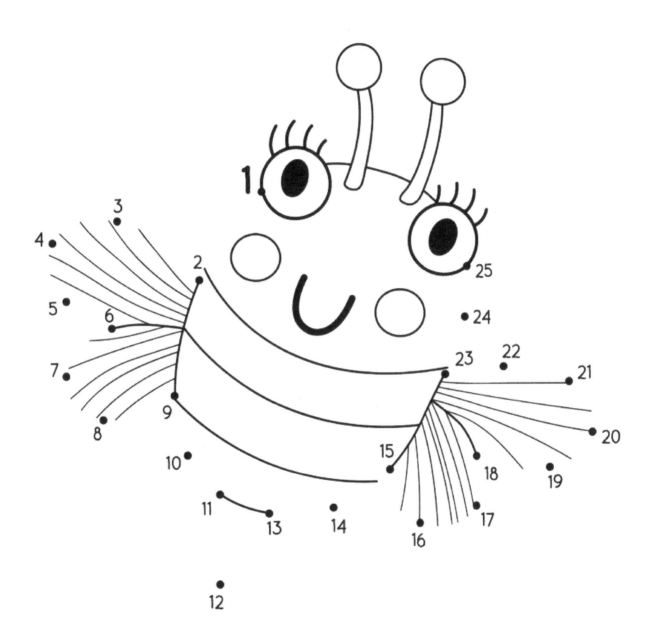

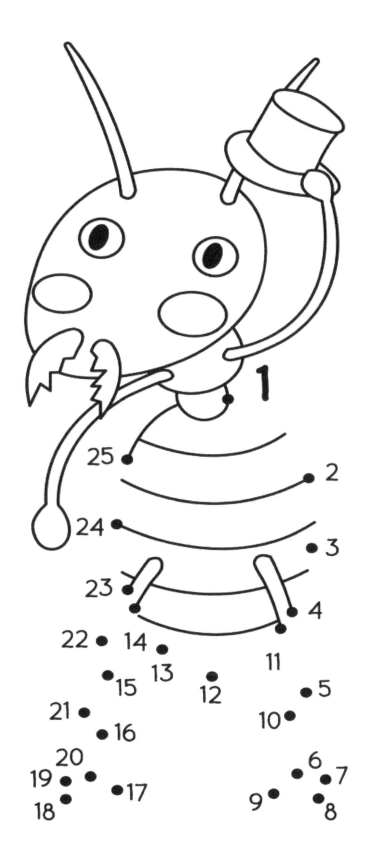

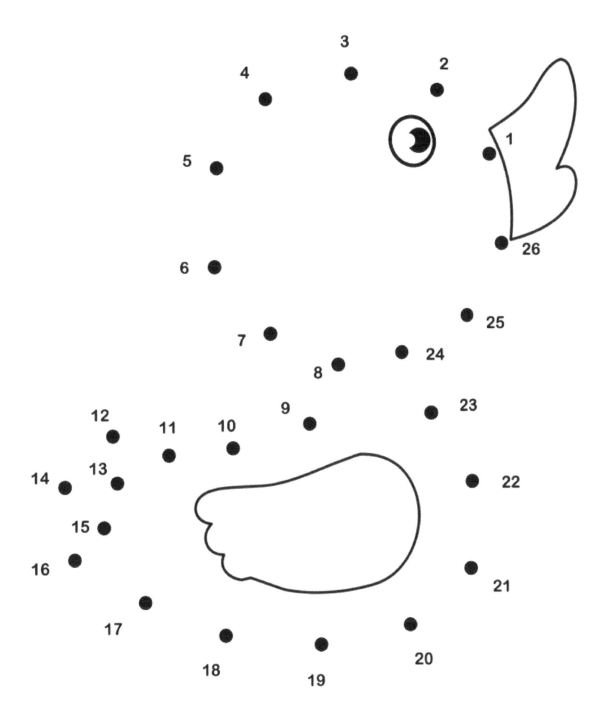

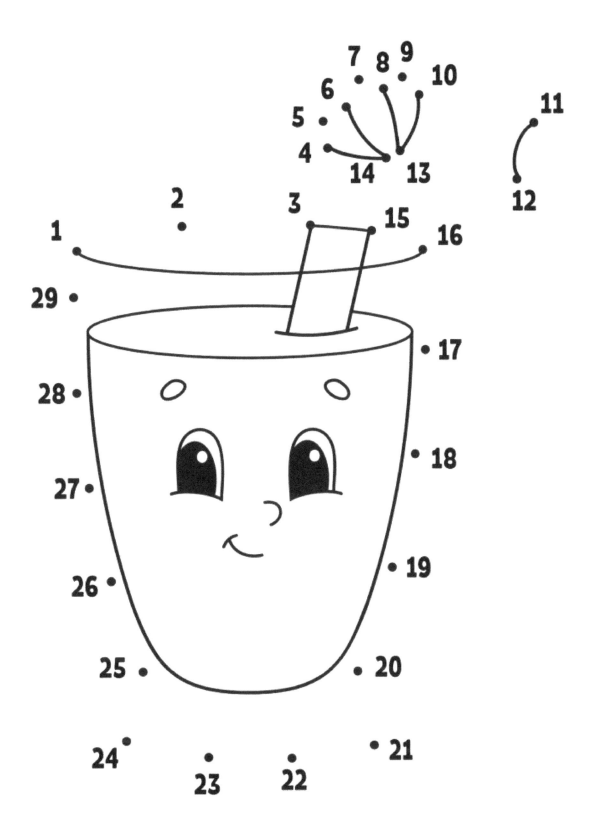

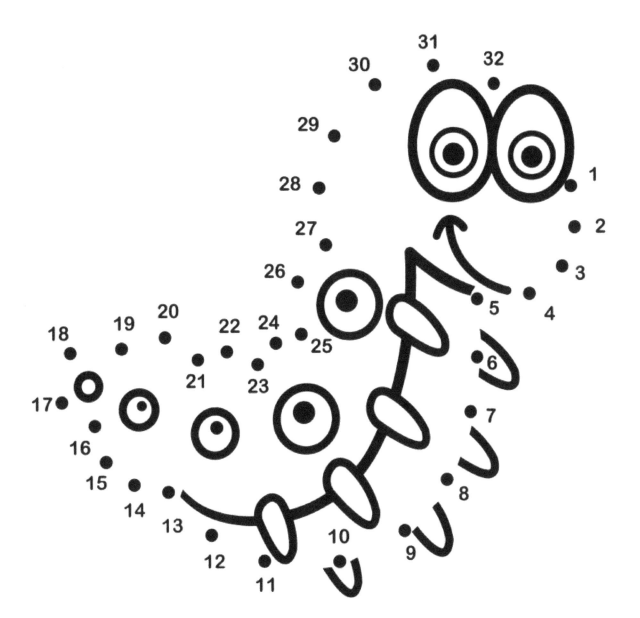

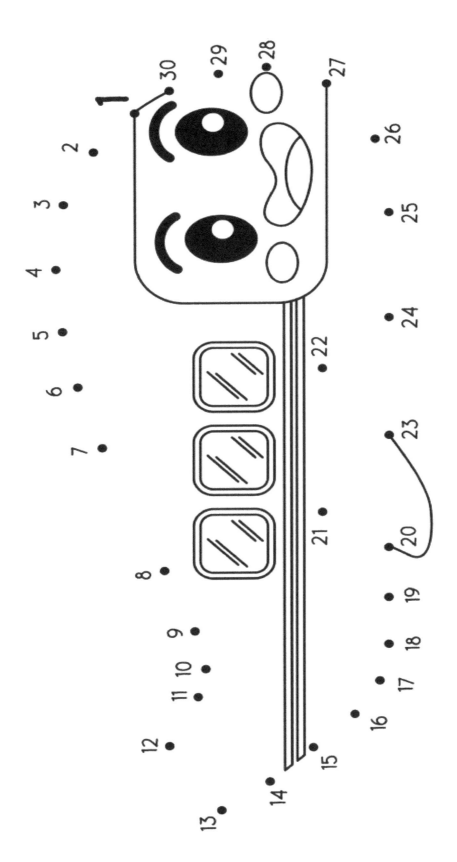

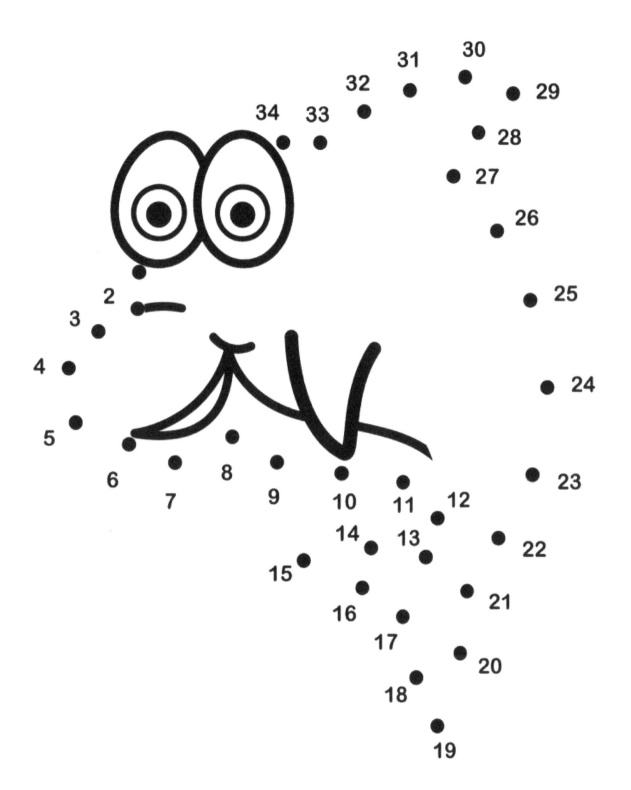

teddy bear	robot	ball
doll	train	kite
car	plane	xylophone

Toys flashcards

building blocks	puzzle	ship
rocking horse	water gun	pinwheel
skateboard	baby rattle	spinning top

Toys flashcards

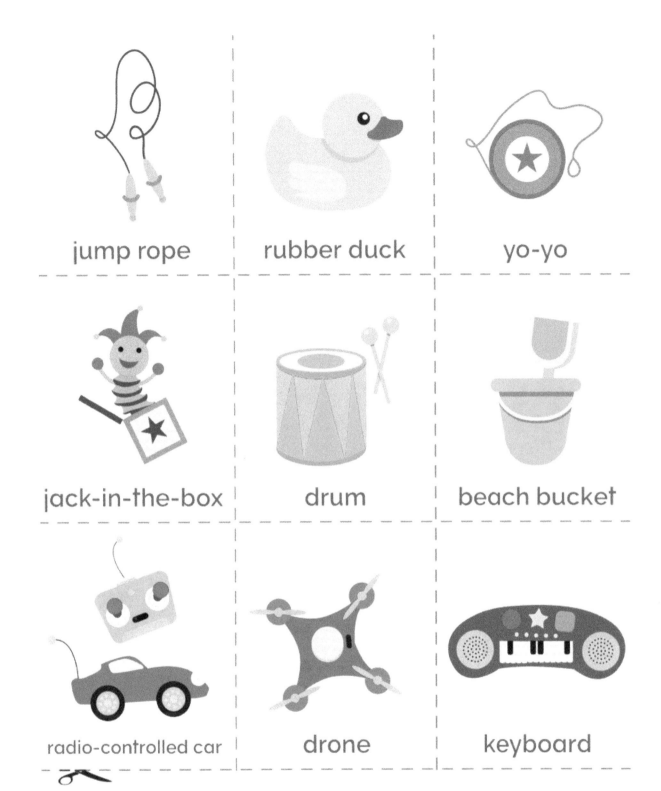

jump rope	rubber duck	yo-yo
jack-in-the-box	drum	beach bucket
radio-controlled car	drone	keyboard

Toys flashcards

In town

- Label the pictures with the correct words from the box below.

> park - station - hospital - school - restaurant
> swimming pool - bridge - church - market

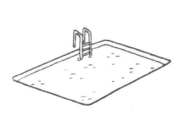

. . . .

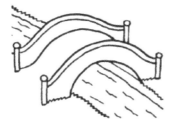

. . . .

. . . .

. . . .

. . . .

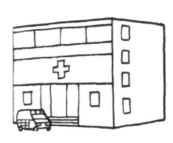

. . . .

. . . .

. . . .

. . . .

In town

• Complete with "there is" or "there isn't".

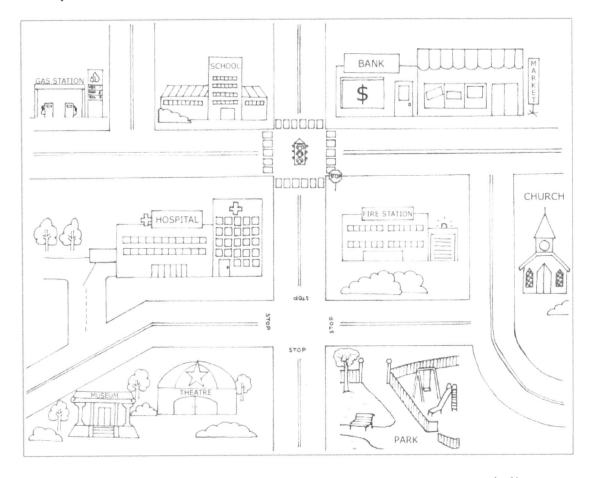

- . . . . a fire station.
- . . . . a library.
- . . . . a museum.
- . . . . a church.
- . . . . a baker's.
- . . . . a bridge.
- . . . . a bank.

- . . . . a gas station.
- . . . . a theatre.
- . . . . a toy shop.
- . . . . a market.
- . . . . a school.
- . . . . a café.
- . . . . a hospital.

Toys

Match the toys to their correct names.

doll

kite

xylophone

water gun

pinwheel

jump rope

teddy bear

jack-in-the-box

radio-controlled car

Toys

Label the pictures with the correct words from the box below.

building blocks - yo-yo - beach bucket - ship - spinning top
rubber duck - skateboard - rocking horse - baby rattle

Body

• Draw a line from each word to the correct part of the body.

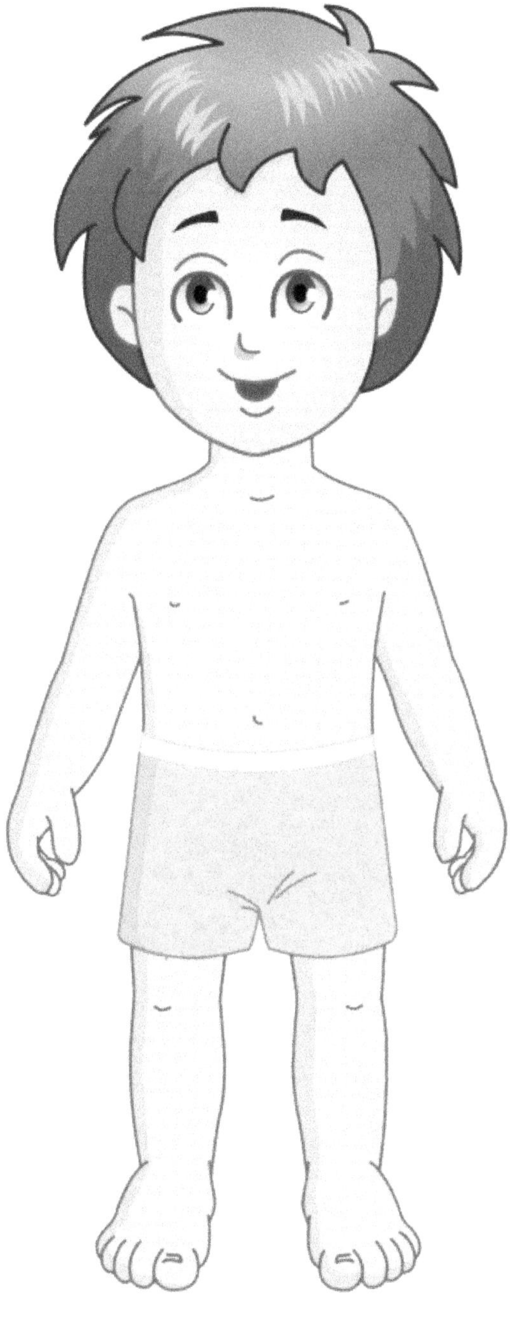

EYE

FOOT

LEG

HAND

NOSE

MOUTH

HEAD

HAIR

ARM

CHEST

NECK

EAR

Body

• Draw a line from each word to the correct part of body.

nose

eyebrow

forehead

eyelid

teeth

mouth

Body

• Draw a line from each word to the correct part of body.

legs

calf

hips

foot

ankel

knees

FIND THE DIFFERENCE

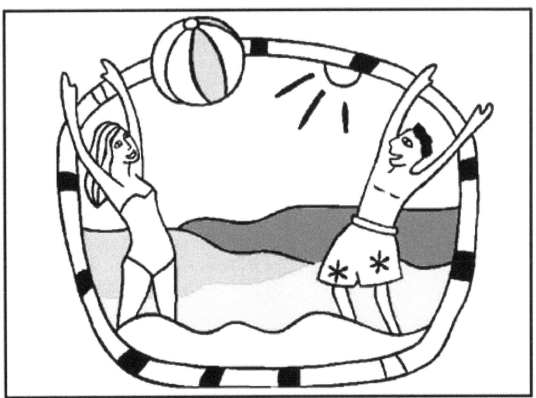

GAME OF SYMMETRY

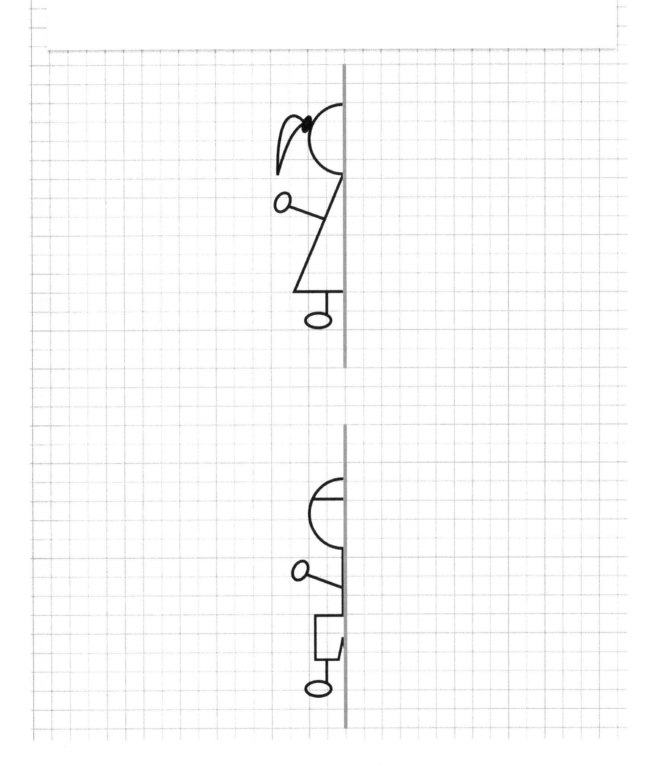

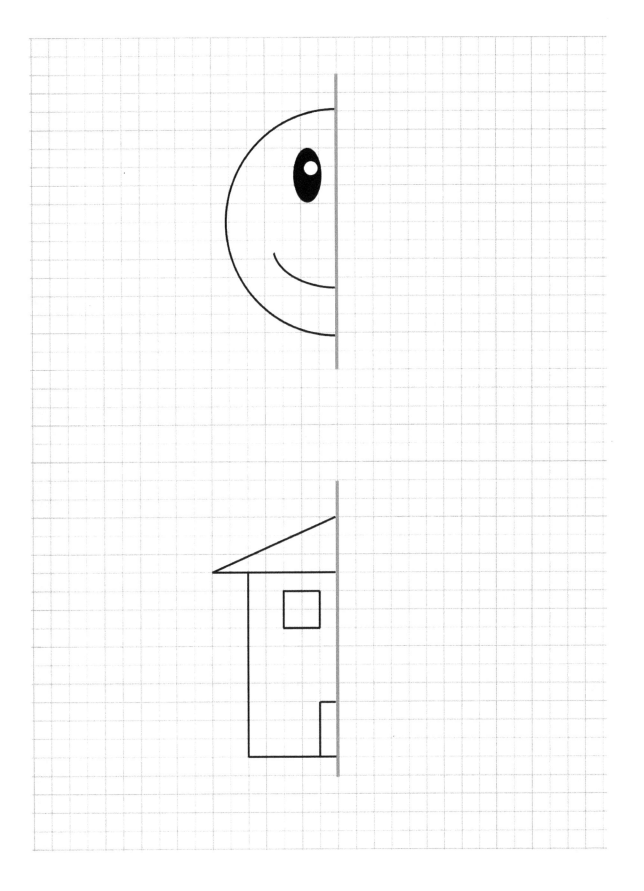

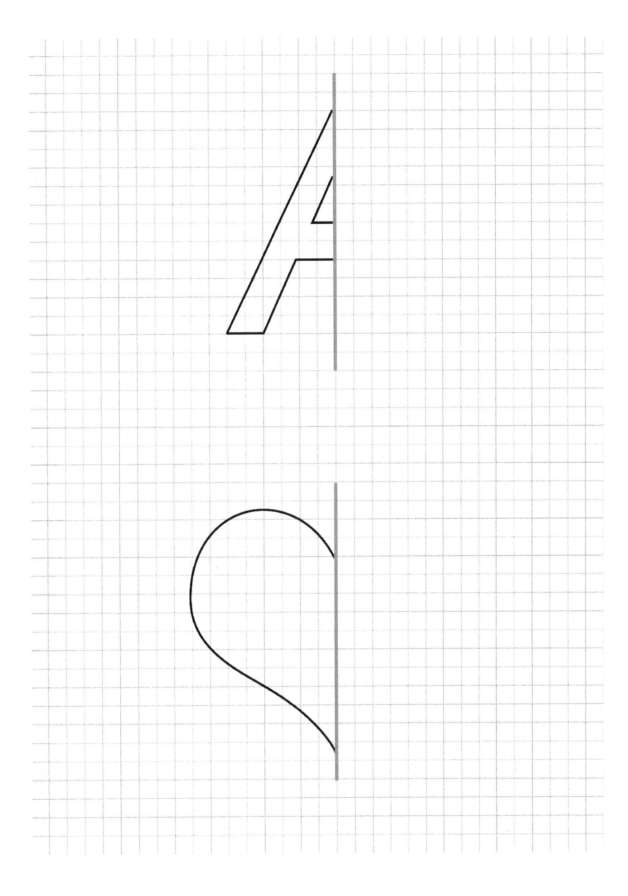

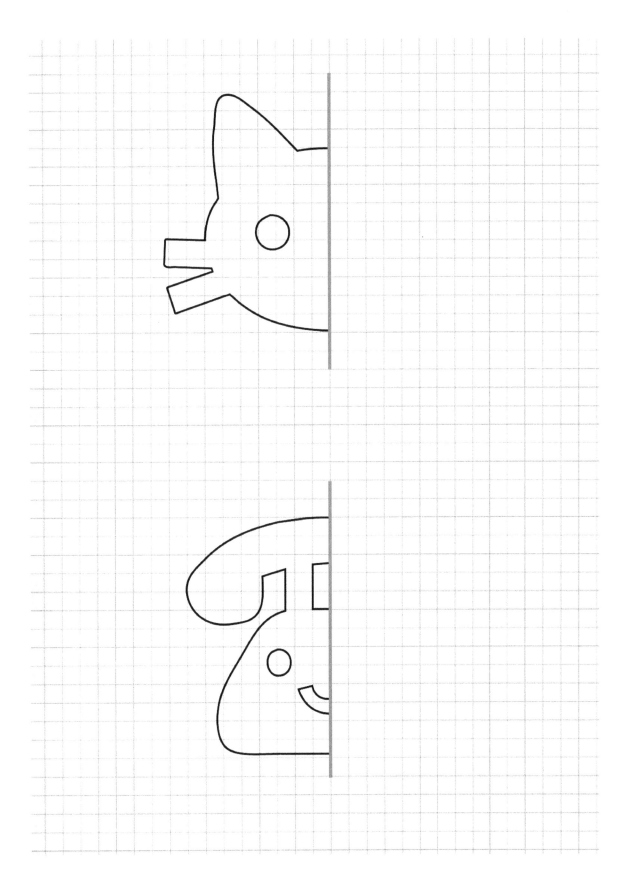

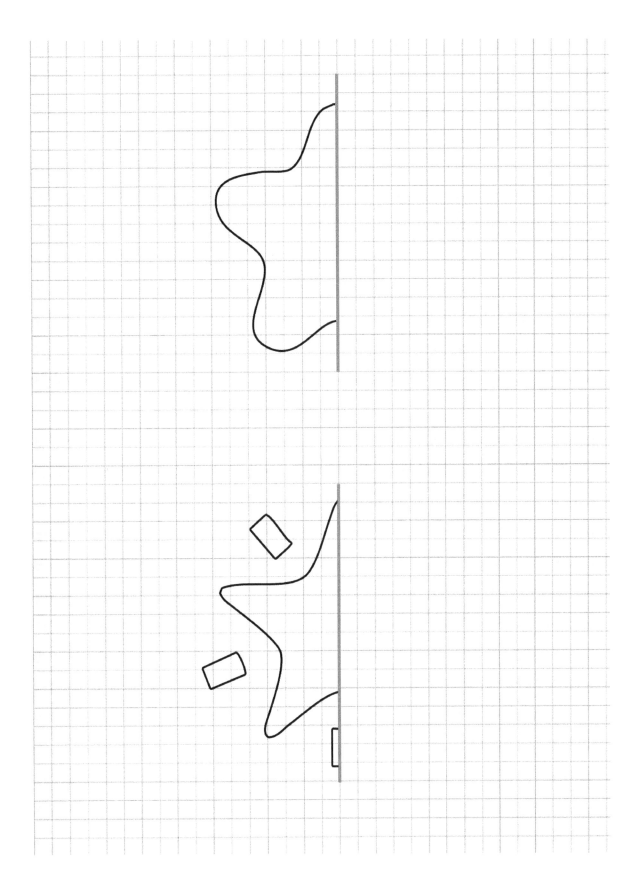

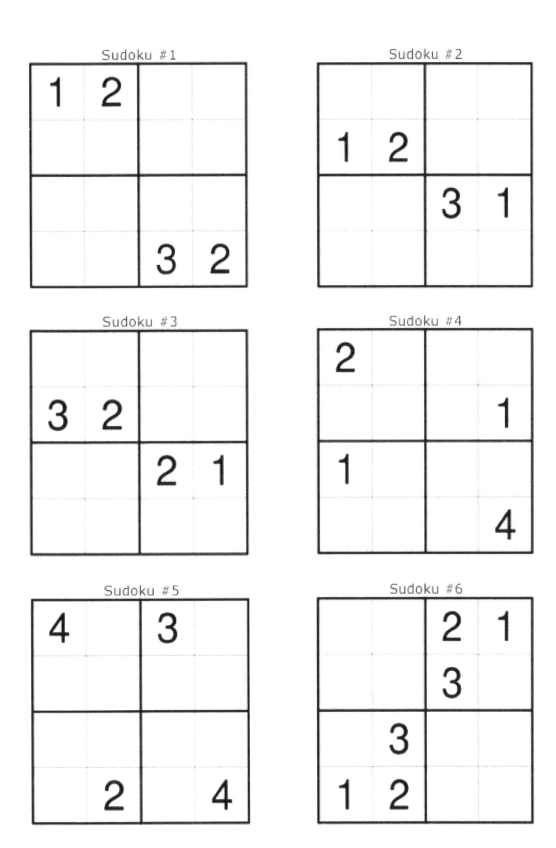

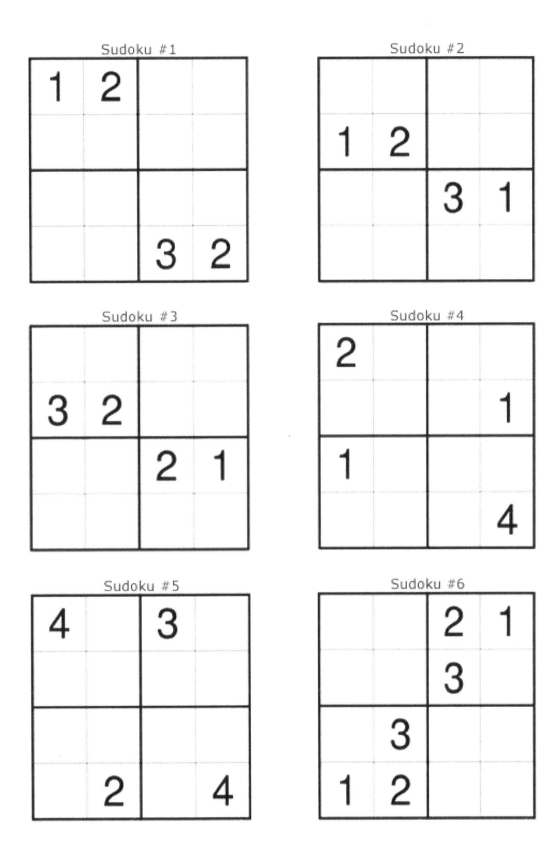

Sudoku #1

Sudoku #2

Sudoku #3

Sudoku #4

Sudoku #5

Sudoku #6

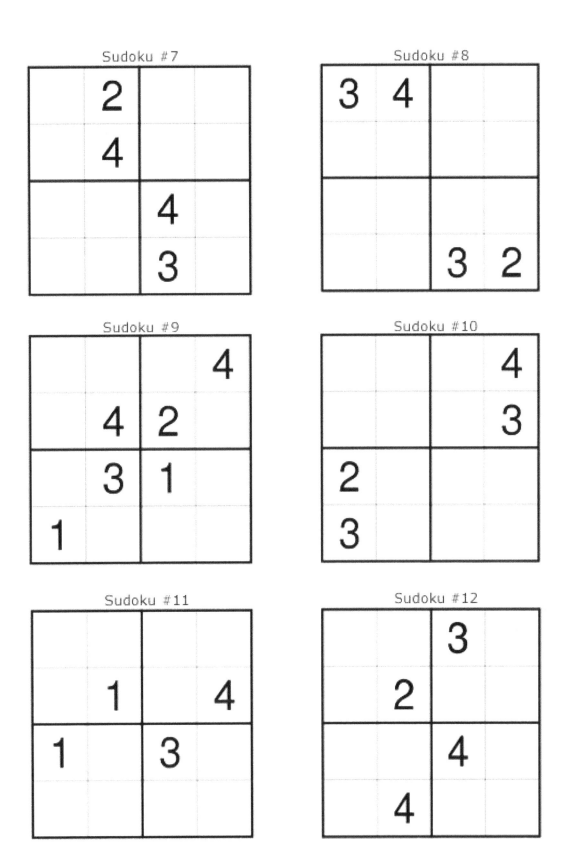

Sudoku #13

		3	1
2	1		

Sudoku #14

	4		
		1	
	3		
			4

Sudoku #15

	1		
		4	
	3		
		1	

Sudoku #16

1	4		
3			
			4
		3	2

Sudoku #17

2			
		1	
	4		
			3

Sudoku #18

			3
1			
			4
3			

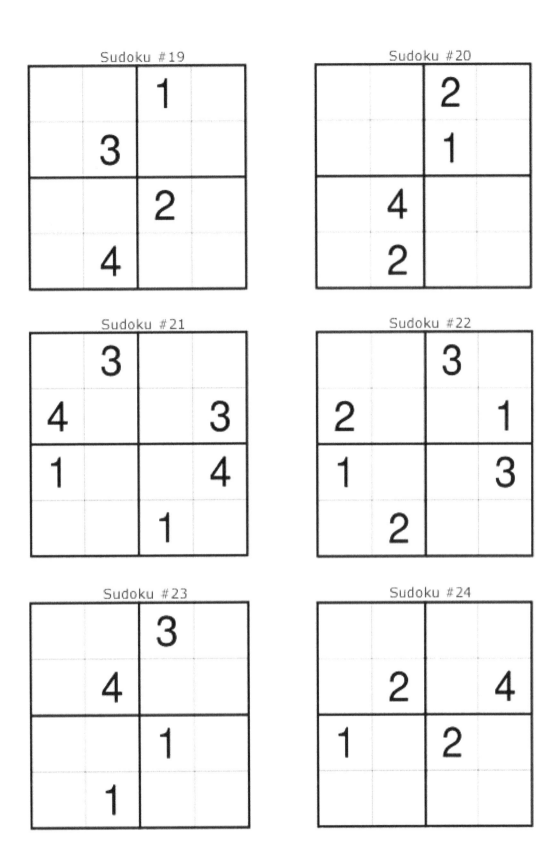

Sudoku #19

Sudoku #20

Sudoku #21

Sudoku #22

Sudoku #23

Sudoku #24

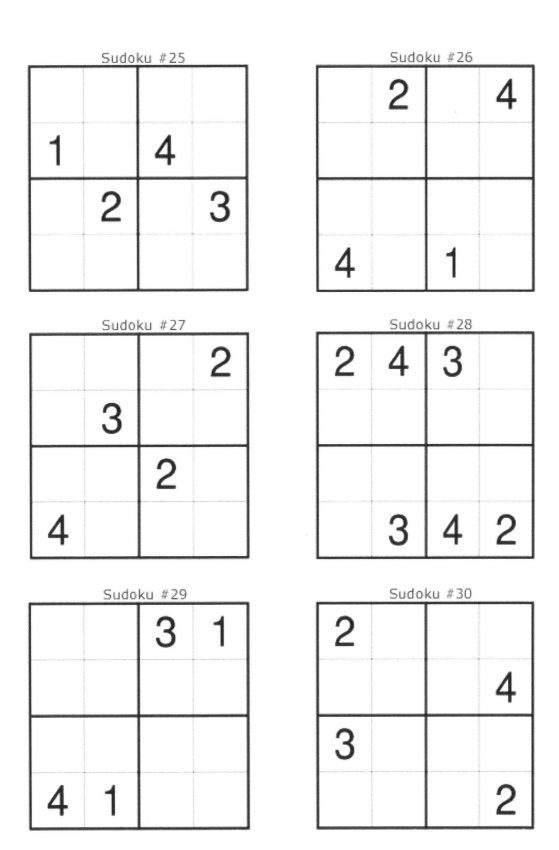

Sudoku #25

Sudoku #26

Sudoku #27

Sudoku #28

Sudoku #29

Sudoku #30

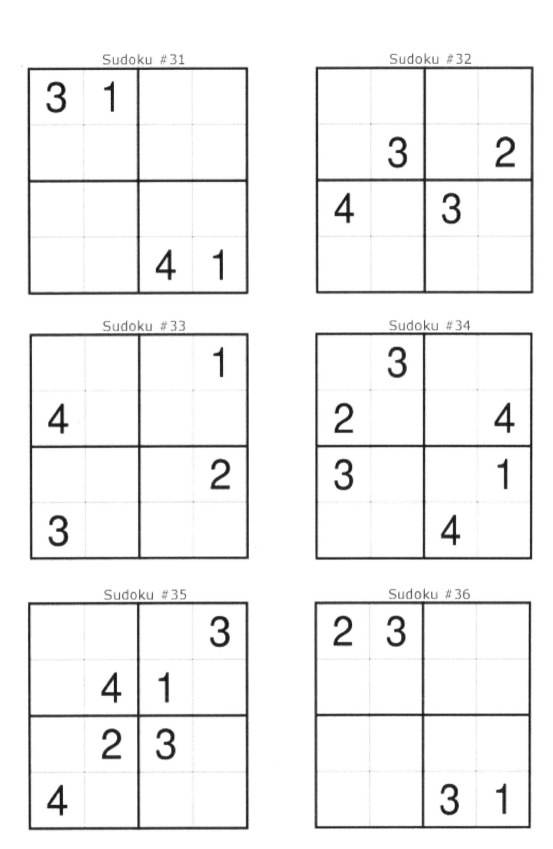

Sudoku #31

Sudoku #32

Sudoku #33

Sudoku #34

Sudoku #35

Sudoku #36

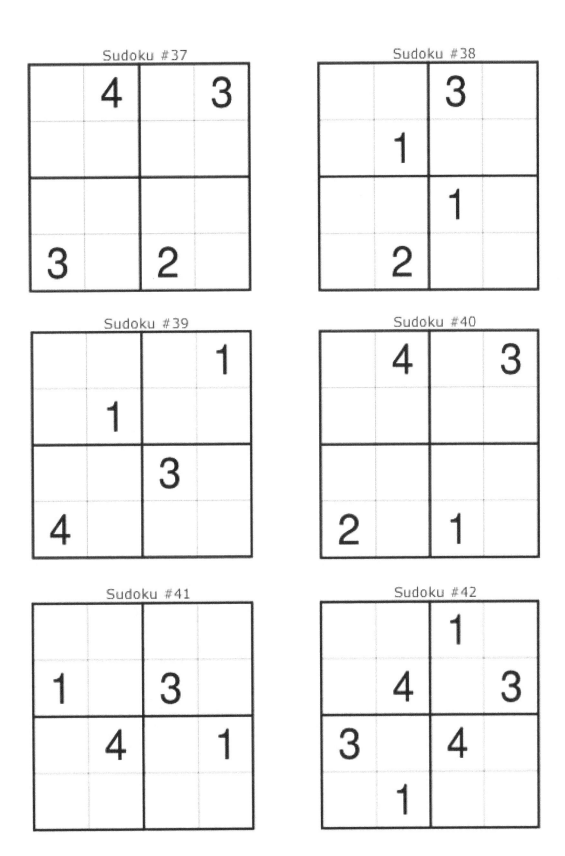

Sudoku #37

Sudoku #38

Sudoku #39

Sudoku #40

Sudoku #41

Sudoku #42

Sudoku #43

		1	
	3		
		2	
	1		

Sudoku #44

1	4		
		2	1

Sudoku #45

3			
1			
			2
			3

Sudoku #46

	4		2
2		1	

Sudoku #47

	1		
		2	
	3		
		1	

Sudoku #48

2	3		
		2	4

Sudoku #49

2			
			4
4			
			3

Sudoku #50

			1
	4		
		3	
2			

Sudoku #51

			3
	2		
		4	
4			

Sudoku #52

2	4		
		3	2

Sudoku #53

4		2	
	1		
		1	
	2		4

Sudoku #54

2			
3			
			2
			1

LABYRINTH

Months of the year

- rewrite the words in correct order

September	
April	
August	
October	
January	
March	
July	
November	
February	
May	
December	
June	

Months of the year

WRITE THE PREVIOUS MONTH

	October	November
	July	August
	March	April
	December	January
	August	September
	June	July
	February	March
	May	June
	January	February
	April	May
	September	October
	November	December

Months of the year

REORDER THE LETTERS AND REWRITE THE CORRECT NAMES

Jarynua	
Faruebry	
Mhcra	
Alipr	
Mya	
Jenu	
Jylu	
Astugu	
Sebremtep	
Obetroc	
Nevermbo	
Dembecer	

Months of the year

WRITE THE NEXT MONTH		
January	February	
April	May	
September	October	
November	December	
August	September	
June	July	
February	March	
May	June	
October	November	
July	August	
March	April	
December	January	